Small Business ₁ ₒₗ
Service Members Book

*Build a Profitable Business By Implementing These
15 Successful Tried & True Revenue Generating
Actions*

Every year small business owners achieve
profitability with their companies, but the number
of these success stories is small relative to the
businesses that become stagnant or fail. What do
the profitable business owners know that others
don't know?

In this revolutionary Itty Bitty® Book, Russ
Barnes shares the steps that countless business
owners have used to create strong revenue
streams and explains HOW to use these steps to
create the lifestyle of your choice.

For example:

- The most important step of all is to
  determine WHY you want to build a
  business. (Step 1)
- Build your team of advisors and develop
  a functional network. (Steps 7 and 9)
- Before you can become purposefully
  profitable, you must accept the fact that
  you are in business to make money. (Step
  12)

**Pick up a copy of this powerful book today
and experience the success of building a
profitable business.**

Your Amazing Itty Bitty® Small Business for Service Members Book

15 Things You Need To Know To Be
Purposefully Profitable

Russ Barnes

Published by Itty Bitty® Publishing
A subsidiary of S & P Productions, Inc.

Printed in the United States of America

Itty Bitty® Publishing
311 Main Street, Suite D
El Segundo, CA 90245
(310) 640-8885

ISBN: 978-0-9987597-9-1

This Itty Bitty® Book is dedicated to all of the small business owners who pour their heart and soul into serving their community with hopes and dreams of building a profitable company. The failure rate is high, but still you drive on.

It's also dedicated to the service members who protect this nation's freedom and security and who strive to continue serving in an entrepreneurial capacity.

Finally, it's dedicated to my family who wonder why I endure this journey when I have the choice to live under more pleasant circumstances.

Stop by our Itty Bitty® website to find more interesting entries regarding Small Business for Service Members……….

www.IttyBittyPublishing.com

Or visit **Russ Barnes** at

www.systro.org

Table of Contents

Introduction

In this book you will find 15 Itty Bitty things you need to know to become purposefully profitable in your small business. The list does not encompass everything you need to know or do; however, it will serve as a guide to help you build your small business into a thriving company.

When I retired from the US Air Force after 27 years of active duty, I was determined to become a successful business owner. I found the challenge to be huge and the guidance to be lacking. The guidance was effective for what it was designed to do, but it didn't help me do what I needed most: To Make Money.

So I set out to determine why the gap existed and to see if anything could be done about it. This book contains the essence of what I learned about building profitable small businesses – both from people who have done it and based on my own experience.

The challenges have not gone away, but armed with this information, you will be able to see the obstacles more clearly and hurdle them more effectively.

Step 1
Clarity

Before you can become purposefully profitable, you must be clear on your purpose. Having clarity on what you intend to achieve helps you articulate your value, take action with energy, and assess your accomplishments along the way.

1. As a service member, you have been trained to assess, adapt and overcome.
2. You've learned teamwork and the power of determination.
3. You've also learned to be comfortable performing in ambiguous environments, with little to no guidance or direction.
4. Building your own business will demand all of these skills.
5. The most important step of all is to determine WHY you want to build a business.
6. Your WHY will be expressed in terms of vision, mission and value.
   a. Vision – What will your life look and feel like from this day forward?
   b. Mission – How will you fulfill your vision?
   c. Value – What will you exchange for the lifestyle of your choosing?

How to Gain Clarity

When I retired from the military, my vision was this: I would NEVER work for anyone EVER again!

I was self-motivated, driven to achieve and committed to fulfilling my purpose…whatever that turned out to be. And for me, the obvious choice was to build a business.

I had clarity on my vision, but I had a lot to learn about mission and value.

- To gain clarity on your vision, mission and value, begin by educating yourself on business through no-to-low-cost educational opportunities and by reading relevant books on business basics.
- Until you gain clarity, ask yourself daily:
  - What do I do well?
  - What type of business requires my skill, talent, experience and abilities?
  - Who will pay for what I can offer?

Resources:

- Small Business Administration courses
- Reading List:
  - The Science of Getting Rich
  - Rich Dad, Poor Dad
  - E-Myth Revisited
  - The Passion Test
  - The 7 Habits of Highly Effective People

Step 2
Marketability

Before you can become purposefully profitable, you must have something to sell. There is no point in building a business until you have proven that people will pay for your product or service.

What you decide to sell must give you pleasure to produce and deliver. Money should not be the main factor; but you must make enough to live the lifestyle of your choice.

To find your marketable value, take several personal and career assessment tests. Include your transferable military skills in the evaluation.

1. Assessment – Often we are asked to do work that does not allow us to perform to our strengths. Now, you can choose your work, but first, you must assess your talent and embrace your strengths.

2. Transferable Military Skills – Your initial military training included a specialty, but over time you were also trained as a teammate, leader, manager and instructor. You learned organization, attention to detail and how to get a job done. These are valuable assets in business.

How to find your Marketability

You've probably heard the statement: "Do what you love and you'll never work a day in your life." I love TV, but no one would pay me to watch it, so I modified the statement to say: Do what you love *that has marketable value* and you'll never work a day in your life.

I found my marketable value by taking a number of personality and career assessments and reading many personal development and business-related books. Finding my marketable value changed everything for me. It was worth the effort.

Resources:

- Personal and career assessments
  - DiSC Profile
  - Myers-Briggs Type Indicator
  - Hollands Self-Directed Search
  - Hermann Brain Dominance Instrument

- Reading List:
  - Strength Finders
  - The Truth About You
  - The Big Idea
  - The Go-Giver
  - Raving Fans

Step 3
Location, Location, Location

Before you can become purposefully profitable, it is important that you understand the dynamics of the location where you choose to start your business.

1. Some locations are better suited for trades, others for technology, some for government-related products and services, and others for hospitality or entertainment.
2. Where you go will have an impact on your ability to find customers at the price point and volume you need to be profitable.
3. Market Environment – there are two business environments that will impact your approach: Transactional and Relational.
   a. In a transactional environment, business is based on what you do.
   b. In a relational environment, business is based on who knows you.
4. Market Infrastructure – the location you choose may drive costs up or down.
   a. Being near key suppliers or far away.
   b. Being near distribution channels or far away.

Consider these factors and others as you evaluate the match between your business and its location.

How to Assess Location

I was cautioned that it would be challenging to build a business in Florida during the time when I started because my business required employees and the labor force was unreliable.

- Confidence caused me to disregard this advice, but I should have taken it.
- The good news is that by starting in that environment, I learned my craft under the most challenging circumstances.
- Choose your location carefully, based on your product or service. Where you start will be a factor in how long it will take to become purposefully profitable.
- Conduct research to identify the best location for the business of your choice.
- If you decide to start your business where you want to live, instead of where the business will thrive, prepare for the possibility that it could take longer to become purposefully profitable.

Resources:

- The Bureau of Labor Statistics
- The Small Business Administration
- The US Census
- Reading List:
    - Blue Ocean Strategy
    - Good to Great

Step 4
Options

Before you can become purposefully profitable,
you must choose the right vehicle. Your choice
will depend on your tolerance for risk, the
resources you have and your experience.

You will have to weigh the opportunities against
what it will cost to get started. Whether you've
retired or separated after an initial tour, you will
have military benefits that will serve you well, if
you apply them wisely.

1. Risk and Resources – Being unprepared
   for battle and lacking firepower put you
   and your team at risk. Being unprepared
   for business and lacking resources puts
   you and your family at risk.
2. Opportunities and Costs - Some business
   opportunities require a small financial
   investment and lots of "sweat equity";
   others require a significant financial
   investment and lots of "business savvy."
3. Experience – It's easy to get in over your
   head very quickly. Choose options that
   will allow you to leverage the personal
   and professional experience that you
   already possess.

How to Assess Options

A legitimate business involves a value-for-value exchange. Evaluate your business opportunities based on whether a product or service is sold for compensation.

- Choose a product or service that you love
- Test your ability to sell it
- Begin where you've had the most success with selling the product or service

Here are some options to consider:
- Direct Sales Business
- Purchase a Franchise
- Purchase an existing business
- Start up a new business

I started out with direct sales (Amway, Market America), progressed to a mobile franchise (Fibrenew) and then to a startup (Systro). My goal at each stage was to earn while I learned.

Resources:

- Reading List:
  - Ultimate Guide to Network Marketing
  - Street Smart Franchising
  - The Prior Service Entrepreneur
  - Ready, Fire, Aim
  - Launch!

Step 5
Strategy

Before you can become purposefully profitable, you must decide what profitability means to you. A strategy is simply what has to happen to get from where you are to where you want to be. So, determining where you want to be is the first step to building an adaptable strategy that includes entry and exit planning.

Every business has barriers to entry and there are only three ways to exit a business—scale, sale or fail.

1. Entry – Plan to overcome barriers to entry, which include competition, the economy and timing, as well as lack of knowledge, experience, and funds.
2. Exit Strategy – As strange as it might sound, it's wise to plan your exit strategy at the very beginning of the process. This will enable you to make the difficult resource management choices.
   a. Scale – build an asset that will serve your family for generations.
   b. Sale – build an asset that will sell within 3-7 years.
   c. Fail – neglect to choose a or b.

How to create Entry and Exit Strategies

Knowledge is power and information is the source of knowledge. The most important task in determining your entry and exit strategy is performing due diligence.

- Entry
  - Research the environment and the business opportunity thoroughly.
  - Be a very careful shepherd of your time and money. Check six!
- Exit
  - If in doubt, choose to scale. It is less risky and you can always choose to sell, if you scale properly.
  - Consult business valuation experts and business brokers to learn, in advance, how to exit effectively.

Resources:

- Reading List:
  - Business Growth Simplified
  - Turn Your Blood, Sweat and Tears into Cash

Step 6
Mentors

Before you can become purposefully profitable, you must be open to guidance from people who have done what you want to do.

First, seek out people who have successfully built a profitable company. When you have clarity on specifically what you want to do, seek out people who have succeeded in your chosen industry.

Mentors can help in two very important areas: personal development and industry knowledge.

1. Personal development precedes business development.
2. Industry knowledge is essential to maximizing limited resources.

How to Find a Mentor

The value of mentors is immeasurable; however, their time and expertise must be respected. If they see potential in you, they will be generous with their assistance. Your success will make them proud. Here are tips for selecting a mentor:

- If you want advice, ask for help. If you want help, ask for advice.
- The best mentors are to be found at charitable events. They have reached a level of success and a stage in life where they are fulfilled by giving back.
- Seek mentors within the community of veterans. They have the added value of having experienced the same challenges you will face during your transition and transformation.

Resources:

- Reading List:
  - The Go-Getter
  - Mentored by a Millionaire
  - How to Win Friends and Influence People

Step 7
Key Advisors

Before you can become purposefully profitable, you need to build a team of advisors. Advisors are experts in their field who will help you make wise choices with your resources. It's very important to select your advisors carefully. There are six basic advisors that I suggest you have on your team. They are:

1. Health advisor
2. Wealth advisor
3. Accountant
4. Banker
5. Insurance agent
6. Attorney

When you've identified the advisors you trust, make them aware of each other. They represent a team when it comes to your success and should work together on your behalf.

How to Choose Advisors

As service members, frequent reassignment meant having to proactively build relationships with service providers in the civilian community where your new military assignment was located.

We learned to ask military friends at the new location which neighborhoods, schools and service providers had the best reputations for working with transient military families.

Follow the same process to identify your business advisors. Ask people who have experience with the types of advisors you need. Interview several advisors in each category to make sure your choice is based on who will work well with you.

Resources:

- Local Business Journals
- Chambers of Commerce
- Toastmasters

Step 8
Team Building

Before you can become purposefully profitable,
you will need to build a team. In the military, you
did not function alone. Teamwork is the main
thing that makes the U.S. military so effective
and we practiced continuously. Do not try to go it
alone in business.

1. Create alliances with people who serve
   the same customers as you do, but with
   products that are different than yours.
2. Create partnerships with people who
   believe what you believe and have the
   same value system.
3. Hire people and put them in a position to
   do what they do best.
4. Build an internship program to help
   develop the next generation of experts in
   your industry.

How to Build a Team

Always be on the lookout for talent. Talent management is your most important role as a CEO. Your team is only as good as the people on it.

Talent management has three components:

- Talent acquisition
- Talent development
- Talent retention

Depending on your resources, you may not be able to pay people to grow your company, but there are ways you can compensate them for providing assistance. I believe that no one should work for free, but value-for-value exchange does not always mean that money changes hands. Here are some options:

- Offer ownership with company shares
- Offer service-in-kind (barter)
- Offer delayed compensation
- Offer commission

Resources:

- Reading List:
  - The Five Dysfunctions of a Team
  - The Great Game of Business
  - Leading Teams

Step 9
Networking

Before you can become purposefully profitable, you must develop a network. People do business with people they know like and trust. Building relationships that result in business is the purpose of networking.

1. Referral marketing, otherwise known as "word of mouth" is based on opportunity.
2. You will receive a referral only if an opportunity presents itself; therefore, the more people who know you, the better your chances of receiving a referral.
3. In a relational business environment, who you know is important, but what's more important is who knows you.
4. Most people have a circle that includes family, friends, new acquaintances and trusted customers and clients.
5. People will refer you to their circle of valued people only if they believe you will deliver at a high level of quality and in the process, make them look good.

How to Network

Building an effective network takes time and must be developed *before* it is needed. To build your network:

- Volunteer in your area of expertise
- Attend local networking events
- Participate in networking groups
- Take courses and training
- Join professional associations
- Give support to non-profits and charities
- Join Boards as an Advisor or Director
- Develop an online presence on LinkedIn, Facebook, Twitter, Instagram and other social media platforms

Resources:

- Reading List:
  - Business by Referral
  - Helping
  - Become a Key Person of Influence

Step 10
Business Model

Before you can become purposefully profitable, you need to know how to connect your most profitable product (MPP) with the most profitable customer (MPC).

This is your business model and describes precisely how you will generate revenue. People will pay to relieve pain or fulfill desire. Your business model demonstrates how your company will deliver what your customers require.

1. Basic equation: MPP + MPC = Revenue
2. In some cases, you may find that your Most Profitable Product is not your best product. In this case, you may choose to market your Most Preferred Product.
3. You may also find that your Most Profitable Customer demands around-the-clock attention, in which case, you may want to market to your Most Preferred Customer.
4. Your business model is the most direct path to profitability and should get ALL of your attention until you create at least one reliable stream of revenue.
5. With a functional business model, you will be able to pay for support services.

How to Build a Business Model

The basic form business model simply describes how your company makes money. MPP + MPC.

The more advanced form gets into more detail and includes several components:
- Value or Unique Selling Proposition
- Customer
- Resources
- Partnerships
- Structure
- Supply Chain
- Costs

Resources:

- Reading List:
  - Business Model Generation
  - Multiple Streams of Income
  - Book Yourself Solid

Step 11
Business Plan

Before you can become purposefully profitable, you may need to raise money, especially if you are pursuing a Sale Strategy. The business plan is the equivalent of a resume for your business and serves as a marketing tool to describe your value proposition to bankers and venture funders.

Components of the business plan:
1. Executive Summary
2. Company Overview
3. Products and Services
4. Market Analysis
5. Strategy and Implementation Summary
6. Commercialization Plan
7. Financial Plan

The business plan should be updated periodically to reflect growth plans and financial projections.

How to Develop a Business Plan

Writing a good business plan requires extensive and intensive market research. Two aspects of the business plan carry significant weight with investors – the management team and financial projections.

- Investors want a management team that has the experience to bring the project to a successful and profitable outcome.
- They also want to know when they will receive the return on their investment.

Investors know that a poor management team will run a great product into the ground, while a great team can take a good product to the moon.

Savvy investors will use rules of thumb to determine if the numbers are in the ballpark. If the numbers are off by orders-of-magnitude, then the entire plan will come into question and reduce the chances that investors will fund the project.

Resources:

- Reading List:
  - Steps to Small Business Startup
  - Business Plan in a Day

Step 12
Financials

Before you can become purposefully profitable, you must accept the fact that you are in business to make money. No other reason.

If you give value and receive nothing in exchange, you're a philanthropist. If you take value and give nothing in exchange, you're a thief. Business is a value-for-value exchange.

Since you are in business to make money, you must always, always, always know your money situation.

1. Check your cash position at the end of every day.
2. Develop a financial projection sheet that enables you to see your "burn rate."
3. Set up a rolling 13-week cash projection.
4. Visualize your company's cash trends.
5. Monitor your receivables.

How to Manage Your Financials

As military service members, we are typically not responsible for budgets. Program and Project Managers have some experience with financials, but in business, nothing is more important.

Here are some tips:
- Build a budget and monitor it
- Know your margins
- Raise prices to account for rising costs
- Learn a financial software such as Quickbooks, Freshbooks, or Xero
- Choose a bookkeeper, accountant and/or tax attorney to advise you. Meet regularly.

Resources:

- Reading List:
    - The Second Decision
    - Simple Numbers, Straight Talk, Big Profits

Step 13
Organization

Before you can become purposefully profitable, you must be organized enough to make the most of your resources in time, money and people.

1. Organization overcomes limitations
2. Systems overcome uncertainty
3. Strategy overcomes impatience
4. Management overcomes complexity
5. Structure influences behavior

Actionable definitions of organization:

1. Being able to find what you need, when you need it. Neat does not equal organized. You can be very neatly disorganized.
2. Knowing what to do and when to do it. Simple, but not easy.
3. Steady progress, in small increments, using a proven process.

How to Organize

Organizing is a continuous process and must be the top priority when productivity is declining.

- If a task is repeatable, create a system.
- Build systems to run the business and bring on people to run the systems.
- Having systems will enable you to delegate effectively. Delegation is the practice of tasking subordinates to use standard operating procedures to handle routine matters, leaving the manager free to handle exceptions.
- In the short term, routine achieves results.

Resources:

- Reading List:
    - Reinventing Organizations
    - Designing Dynamic Organizations
    - Organizational Physics

Step 14
Pitfalls

Before you can become purposefully profitable, you must be aware of the pitfalls that may derail your enterprise. Two pitfalls that trip up military service members are overconfidence and overextending.

1. Overconfidence – Many service members believe that their military experience has prepared them to do everything with nothing and in no time at all.
2. Overextending – Business happens according to its own clock and you will need to pace your effort and deploy your resources carefully in order to remain in sync with the tempo of the environment.

How to Avoid Pitfalls

Whether you are running a large business or small business, there is a progression that you must understand in order to make the best use of your resources.

Become familiar with this progression and use it to make the right decisions and take the right actions in the right order, with the right timing:
- Personal Development - education
- Product Development – business model
- Platform Development - visibility
- Business Development - sales
- Market Development - growth
- Organization Development - structure

This progression is not a checklist, but getting out of sync in the framework without a logical reason could be costly in terms of time and money.

Resources:

- Reading List:
  - Scaling Up
  - The Fifth Discipline
  - E-Myth Mastery

Step 15
Success Secret

Before you can become purposefully profitable, you must have such passion for what you do that the idea of *not* doing it is unimaginable. Believe that you can be the best in the world at it.

Military service members suffer from three challenges that make it difficult for us to achieve the success that we are very capable of achieving:

1. We struggle to articulate precisely what we want to do, believing that we can do anything with nothing, in no time at all.
2. We struggle with promoting ourselves as individuals, having been exposed to the amazing benefits of working with a team.
3. We struggle to request compensation in accordance with the value we deliver.

The secret to success as a small business owner is focus. Concentrate on doing what you do best in a way that helps the most people possible.

1. The Law of Compensation – Your income is determined by how many people you serve and how well you serve them.
2. "You can get what you want by helping people get what they want" – Zig Ziglar

How to Leverage the Success Secret

The guidance in this book provides what you need to know to become purposefully profitable. Use the knowledge to create value-for-value exchanges and live the life that you choose.

- Be passionate for your craft. Passion will energize you and inspire you. Passion is contagious and the people who believe what you believe will join your team.
- Never stop learning.
- The life of an entrepreneur is fun, challenging, frustrating, rewarding, uplifting, depressing and fulfilling.
- Building a small business is not for the faint of heart. The good news is, through military training, you have cultivated the mental toughness and intestinal fortitude needed to grow a profitable business.

You have been proven worthy. Go forth and conquer!

Resources:

- Reading List:
  - Peak Performers
  - The 80/20 Principle
  - Conscious Capitalism
  - Firms of Endearment

You've finished. Before you go...

Tweet/share that you finished this book.

Please star rate this book.

Reviews are solid gold to writers. Please take a few minutes to give us some itty bitty feedback.

ABOUT THE AUTHOR

Colonel (retired) Russ Barnes is the CEO and Senior Business Advisor to Entrepreneurs and Executives at Systro, an organization design firm specializing in small business development. He has more than 30 years of experience in organization development drawn from military service, franchise ownership, academic programs and strategy consulting, specifically with small businesses.

Russ flew combat missions as a B-52 Radar Navigator during Desert Storm and later held senior leadership positions in several higher headquarters staff organizations, which included the Pentagon and three Combatant Commands.

After retirement from the military, Russ purchased a franchise and grew it from zero to profitability in less than three years. His growth was based on a clear vision, an effective network, consistently delivering a quality product and maintaining a keen focus on customer service.

Russ received his Bachelor's Degree from Manhattan College (NY), his MBA from Embry-Riddle Aeronautical University, and his Master of Science degree in Strategic Studies from Air University.

www.systro.org

If you liked this Itty Bitty® book you might also enjoy...

- **Your Amazing Itty Bitty® Veterans Survival Book** – Earl J. Katigbak

- **Your Amazing Itty Bitty® Going Home Book** –Carolyn R. Owens

- **Your Amazing Itty Bitty® Little Black Book of Sales** – Anthony Camacho

Or many other Itty Bitty® books available online.